devotion
newsboys

2	devotion
9	i love Your ways
18	presence (my heart's desire)
24	strong tower
30	God of nations
36	blessed be Your name
46	the orphan
55	landslide of love
65	Name above all names
71	when the tears fall

ISBN 0-634-09522-6

7777 W. BLUEMOUND RD. P.O. BOX 13819 MILWAUKEE, WI 53213

For all works contained herein:
Unauthorized copying, arranging, adapting, recording or public performance is an infringement of copyright.
Infringers are liable under the law.

Visit Hal Leonard Online at
www.halleonard.com

DEVOTION

Words and Music by PETER FURLER
and STEVE TAYLOR

© 2004 ARIOSE MUSIC and SOYLENT TUNES
ARIOSE MUSIC Admin. by EMI CMG PUBLISHING
SOYLENT TUNES Admin. by ICG
All Rights Reserved   Used by Permission

12

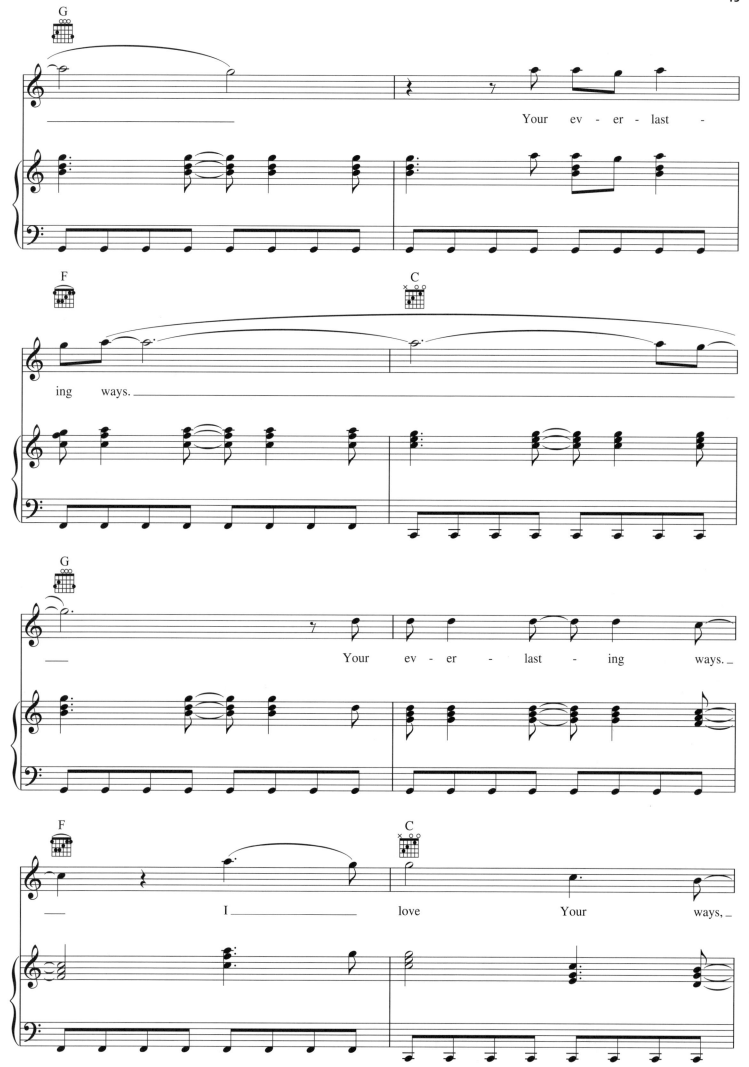

PRESENCE
(My Heart's Desire)

Words and Music by PETER FURLER,
TIM HUGHES and STEVE TAYLOR

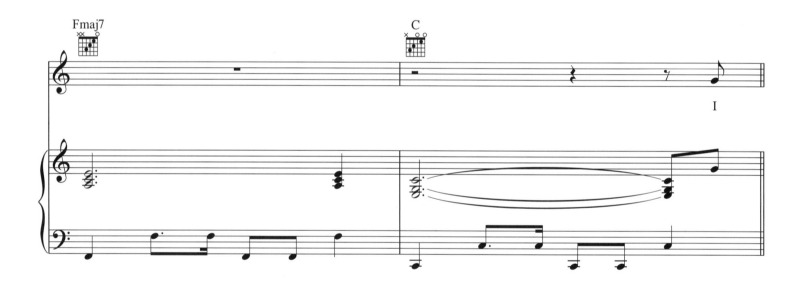

*Recorded a half step higher.

© 2004 ARIOSE MUSIC, THANKYOU MUSIC and SOYLENT TUNES
ARIOSE MUSIC Admin. by EMI CMG PUBLISHING
THANKYOU MUSIC Admin. Worldwide excluding the UK and Europe by WORSHIPTOGETHER.COM SONGS
THANKYOU MUSIC Admin. in the UK and Europe by KINGSWAY MUSIC
SOYLENT TUNES Admin. by ICG
All Rights Reserved   Used by Permission

STRONG TOWER

Words and Music by PETER FURLER
and STEVE TAYLOR

© 2004 ARIOSE MUSIC and SOYLENT TUNES
ARIOSE MUSIC Admin. by EMI CMG PUBLISHING
SOYLENT TUNES Admin. by ICG
All Rights Reserved   Used by Permission

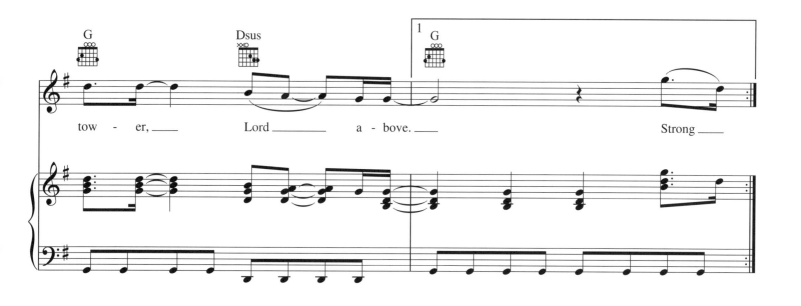
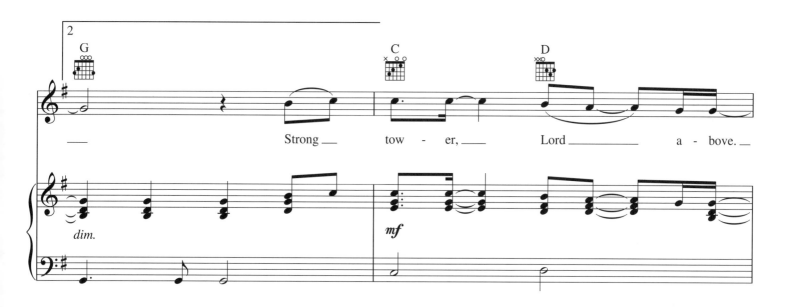
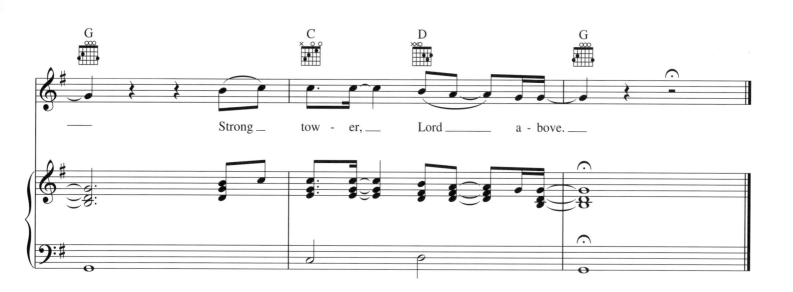

GOD OF NATIONS

Words and Music by PETER FURLER
and STEVE TAYLOR

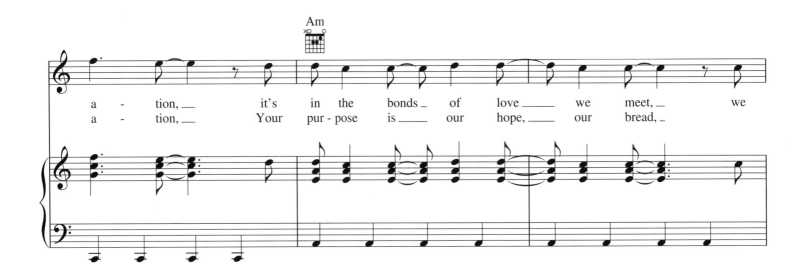

© 2004 ARIOSE MUSIC and SOYLENT TUNES
ARIOSE MUSIC Admin. by EMI CMG PUBLISHING
SOYLENT TUNES Admin. by ICG
All Rights Reserved   Used by Permission

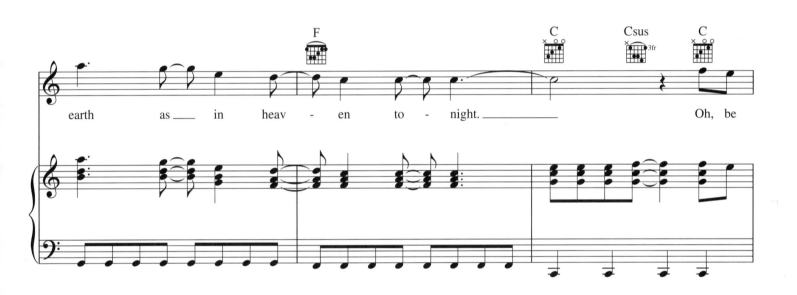
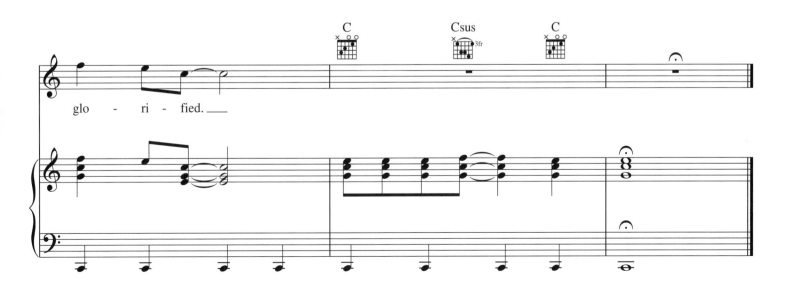

BLESSED BE YOUR NAME

Words and Music by MATT REDMAN
and BETH REDMAN

© 2002 THANKYOU MUSIC (PRS)
Admin. Worldwide excluding the UK and Europe by WORSHIPTOGETHER.COM SONGS
Admin. in the UK and Europe by KINGSWAY MUSIC
All Rights Reserved   Used by Permission

LANDSLIDE OF LOVE

Words and Music by PETER FURLER, STEVE TAYLOR and JEFF FRANKENSTEIN

© 2004 ARIOSE MUSIC, SOYLENT TUNES and OINCH MUSIC
ARIOSE MUSIC Admin. by EMI CMG PUBLISHING
SOYLENT TUNES Admin. by ICG
All Rights Reserved   Used by Permission

NAME ABOVE ALL NAMES

Words and Music by
TIM HUGHES

*Recorded a half step lower.

© 2004 THANKYOU MUSIC (PRS)
Admin. Worldwide excluding the UK and Europe by WORSHIPTOGETHER.COM SONGS
Admin. in the UK and Europe by KINGSWAY MUSIC
All Rights Reserved   Used by Permission

WHEN THE TEARS FALL

Words and Music by
TIM HUGHES

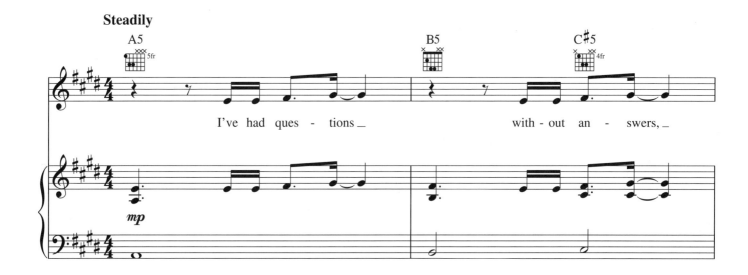

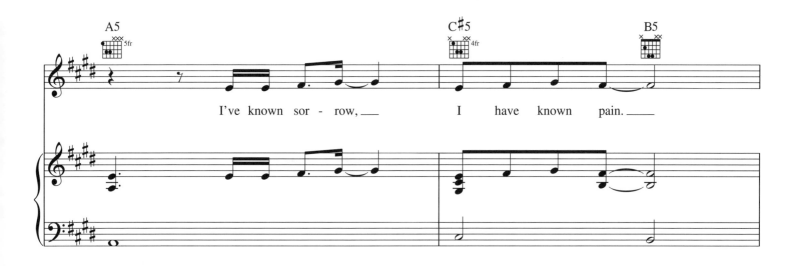

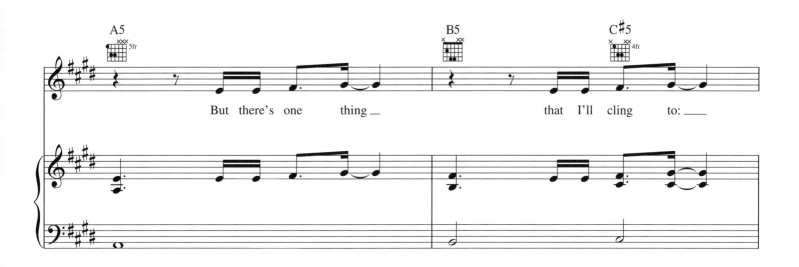

© 2004 THANKYOU MUSIC (PRS)
Admin. Worldwide excluding the UK and Europe by WORSHIPTOGETHER.COM SONGS
Admin. in the UK and Europe by KINGSWAY MUSIC
All Rights Reserved Used by Permission

73

More Contemporary Christian Folios from Hal Leonard
Arranged for Piano, Voice and Guitar

AVALON – THE CREED
Our matching folio to the latest from this popular CCM vocal quartet features photos and all ten songs: Abundantly • All • Be with You • The Creed • Far Away from Here • The Good Way • I Bring It to You • Overjoyed • Renew Me • You Were There.
00306601 .... $16.95

JEREMY CAMP – STAY
The *All Music Guide* says CCM newcomer Jeremy Camp "delivers one of the most awe-inspiring performances of any debut CCM artist in the past decade" and calls *Stay* "vocally, musically and lyrically…a potent mix of one standout cut after another." Our matching folio features all 12 tracks: All the Time • Breaking My Fall • In Your Presence • Nothing • Right Here • Stay • Take My Life • Understand • Walk by Faith • and more.
00306565 .... $16.95

CASTING CROWNS
Matching folio to the Steven Curtis Chapman-produced eponymous debut from this pop/rock band. Features 10 songs: American Dream • Glory • Here I Go Again • If We Are the Body • Life of Praise • Praise You with the Dance • Voice of Truth • What If His People Prayed • Who Am I • Your Love Is Extravagant.
00306621 .... $14.95

STEVEN CURTIS CHAPMAN – ALL THINGS NEW
Matching folio to the latest release from this perennial CCM favorite and multi-Dove Award winner. 12 songs, including: All Things New • Angels Wish • Believe Me Now • The Big Story • Coming Attractions • I Believe in You • Last Day on Earth • Much of You • Only Getting Started • Please Only You • Treasure of Jesus • What Now.
00306662 .... $14.95

DC TALK – INTERMISSION: THE GREATEST HITS
17 of DC Talk's best: Between You and Me • Chance • Colored People • Consume Me • Hardway (Remix) • I Wish We'd All Been Ready • In the Light • Jesus Freak • Jesus Is Just Alright • Luv Is a Verb • Mind's Eye • My Will • Say the Words • Socially Acceptable • SugarCoat It • Supernatural • What If I Stumble.
00306414 .... $14.95

For More Information, See Your Local Music Dealer, Or Write To:

7777 W. Bluemound Rd. P.O. Box 13819 Milwaukee, WI 53213

For a complete listing of the products we have available, Visit us online at **www.halleonard.com**

JEFF DEYO – LIGHT
13 songs from Deyo's second solo release: As I Lift You Up • Bless the Lord • I Am Yours Forever • I Fear You • I Love You • Keep My Heart • Ray of Light • Sacrifice of Praise • Show the Wonder • Take Me to You • These Hands • We Come to Your Throne • Your Name Is Holy.
00306603 .... $14.95

BETHANY DILLON
All 11 songs from the self-titled Sparrow CD from this critically acclaimed 15-year-old singer/songwriter: Aimless • All I Need • Beautiful • Exodus • For My Love • Great Big Mystery • Lead Me On • Move Forward • Revolutionaries • A Voice Calling Out • Why.
00306636 .... $14.95

KEITH GREEN – THE ULTIMATE COLLECTION
This collection matches Sparrow's compilation CD of the late Keith Green, who died in a plane crash in 1982. 20 songs: I Want to Be More Like Jesus • Make My Life a Prayer to You • Oh Lord, You're Beautiful • There Is a Redeemer • You Are the One • more.
00306518 .... $16.95

Songs from
!HERO THE ROCK OPERA
15 selections from the musical that asks, "What if Jesus had been born in Bethlehem…Pennsylvania?" Our collection from this modern-day version of the greatest story ever told includes 15 songs by popular CCM artists: Fire of Love • Hero • I Am • Kill the Hero • Lose My Life with You • Manna from Heaven • Raised in Harlem • Secrets of the Heart • and more.
00306634 .... $14.95

JENNIFER KNAPP – THE COLLECTION
Our songbook matching the greatest hits collection from this alternative CCM folk-rocker: Breathe on Me • By and By • Diamond in the Rough • Hold Me Now • Into You • Lay It Down • A Little More • Martyrs & Thieves • Refine Me • Romans • Say Won't You Say • Undo Me • The Way I Am • When Nothing Satisfies • Whole Again.
00306623 .... $14.95

NICHOLE NORDEMAN – WOVEN & SPUN
Includes all 11 songs from Nordeman's 2002 release: Doxology • Even Then • Gratitude • Healed • Holy • I Am • Legacy • Mercies New • My Offering • Never Loved You More • Take Me As I Am.
00306494 .... $16.95

TWILA PARIS – HOUSE OF WORSHIP
Includes 12 songs: Christ in Us • Come Emmanuel • Fill My Heart • For Eternity • Glory and Honor • God of All • I Want the World to Know • Make Us One • Not My Own • We Bow Down • We Will Glorify • You Are God.
00306517 .... $14.95

PHILLIPS, CRAIG AND DEAN – LET YOUR GLORY FALL
Our matching folio features all ten inspirational tunes from this popular CCM trio's 2003 release: Every Day • Fall Down • Hallelujah (Your Love Is Amazing) • Here I Am to Worship • How Deep the Father's Love for Us • Lord, Let Your Glory Fall • My Praise • Only You • What Kind of Love Is This • The Wonderful Cross.
00306519 .... $14.95

WAIT FOR ME – THE BEST FROM REBECCA ST. JAMES
Our matching folio to the first best-of compilation from Aussie artist Rebecca St. James includes 16 previously recorded songs: Breathe • God • Here I Am • I Thank You • Lamb of God • Mirror • Pray • Psalm 139 • Reborn • Song of Love • Speak to Me • Stand • Wait for Me • and more.
00306546 .... $14.95

SWITCHFOOT – THE BEAUTIFUL LETDOWN
All 11 songs from the CD by these San Diego-based Christian alt-rockers: Adding to the Noise • Ammunition • Beautiful Letdown • Dare You to Move • Gone • Meant to Live • More Than Fine • On Fire • Redemption Side • This Is Your Life • Twenty-Four.
00306547 .... $16.95

THIRD DAY – WIRE
13 songs: Billy Brown • Blind • Come On Back to Me • I Believe • I Got a Feeling • I Will Hold My Head High • Innocent • It's a Shame • Rock Star • San Angelo • 'Til the Day I Die • Wire • You Are Mine.
00306629 .... $14.95

ZOEGIRL – DIFFERENT KIND OF FREE
Our matching folio features all 11 songs: Beautiful Name • Contagious • Different Kind of Free • Feel Alright • Inside Out • Life to Me • Love Me for Me • She • Unbroken • Wait • You Get Me.
00306562 .... $14.95

Prices, contents and availability subject to change without notice.